SCIENCE **BASICS**

WHAT IS MAGNETISM?

by Mark Weakland

a Capstone company—publishers for children
www.raintree.co.uk

Raintree is an imprint of Capstone Global Library Limited, a company incorporated in England and Wales having its registered office at 264 Banbury Road, Oxford, OX2 7DY – Registered company number: 6695582

www.raintree.co.uk
myorders@raintree.co.uk

Text © Capstone Global Library Limited 2019
The moral rights of the proprietor have been asserted.

All rights reserved. No part of this publication may be reproduced in any form or by any means (including photocopying or storing it in any medium by electronic means and whether or not transiently or incidentally to some other use of this publication) without the written permission of the copyright owner, except in accordance with the provisions of the Copyright, Designs and Patents Act 1988 or under the terms of a licence issued by the Copyright Licensing Agency, Barnard's Inn, 86 Fetter Lane, London, EC4A 1EN (www.cla.co.uk). Applications for the copyright owner's written permission should be addressed to the publisher.

Edited by Jaclyn Jaycox and Mari Bolte
Designed by Kyle Grentz
Original illustrations © Capstone Global Library Limited 2019
Picture research by Eric Gohl
Production by Laura Manthe
Originated by Capstone Global Library Ltd
Printed and bound in India

ISBN 978 1 4747 7086 6 (hardback)
23 22 21 20 19
10 9 8 7 6 5 4 3 2 1

ISBN 978 1 4747 7090 3 (paperback)
24 23 22 21 20
10 9 8 7 6 5 4 3 2 1

British Library Cataloguing in Publication Data
A full catalogue record for this book is available from the British Library.

Acknowledgements
We would like to thank the following for permission to reproduce photographs: Alamy: Henry Westheim Photography, 15; Capstone Studio: Karon Dubke, 20–21; Shutterstock: Brian Goodman, 5, haryigit, 9 (top), J. Lekavicius, 17, Jakinnboaz, 11 (bottom), Nilobon Sweeney, 9 (bottom), Pixel 4 Images, 19, saicle, background (throughout), ShutterStockStudio, cover, 7, Valentyn Volkov, 11 (top), worradirek, 13.

Every effort has been made to contact copyright holders of material reproduced in this book. Any omissions will be rectified in subsequent printings if notice is given to the publisher.

All the internet addresses (URLs) given in this book were valid at the time of going to press. However, due to the dynamic nature of the internet, some addresses may have changed, or sites may have changed or ceased to exist since publication. While the author and publisher regret any inconvenience this may cause readers, no responsibility for any such changes can be accepted by either the author or the publisher.

CONTENTS

An invisible force **4**
Push and pull **6**
Types of magnets **8**
Magnetic poles **10**
Magnetic materials **12**
Travel on a maglev train **14**
Electric cars **16**
Making noise **18**
Magnetism experiment **20**

Glossary 22
Find out more 23
Comprehension questions 24
Index 24

AN INVISIBLE FORCE

What can make things move but cannot be seen? It's not magic. It's **magnetism**.

Magnetism is a force. It can pull and push on objects. But the force is invisible. Let's find out more about magnetism and how it works.

magnetism natural force of a magnet, which pulls it to iron or steel

PUSH AND PULL

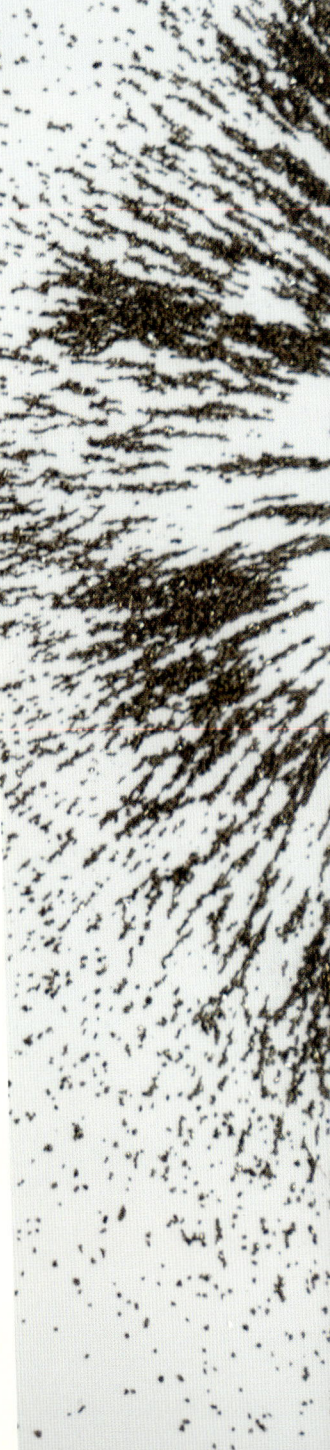

Magnetism comes from electrical **currents**. A current is the flow of electrical charges, such as **electrons**, through an object. The movement of these charges makes a **magnetic field**. A magnetic field around a magnet can create a force on objects in that area.

current movement of electrical charges in a certain direction
electron one of the tiny particles that makes up an atom
magnetic field area around a magnet or electrical current that can produce a force on other objects

SEEING INVISIBILITY

Iron filings make it possible to see the outline of a magnetic field. Small pieces of iron scattered around a magnet line up in the invisible field.

TYPES OF MAGNETS

There are two basic types of magnets. A temporary magnet is made with electricity. This magnet can be turned on and off. A permanent magnet does not need electricity. Its magnetism is always working. A nail is an example of an object that can be made into a temporary magnet. A fridge magnet is a permanent magnet.

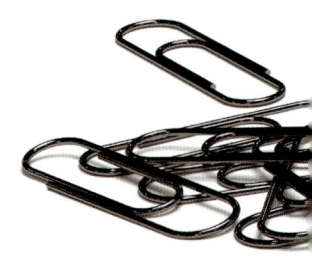
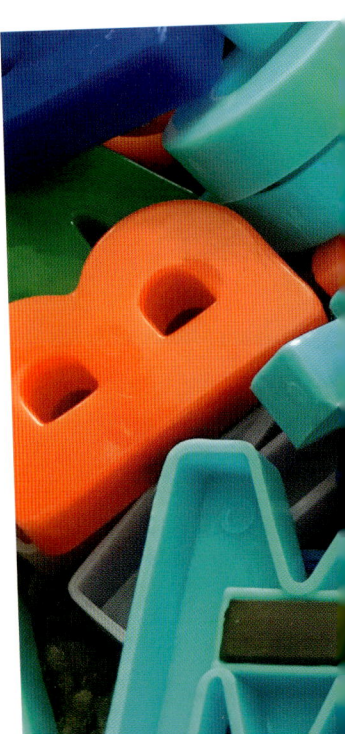

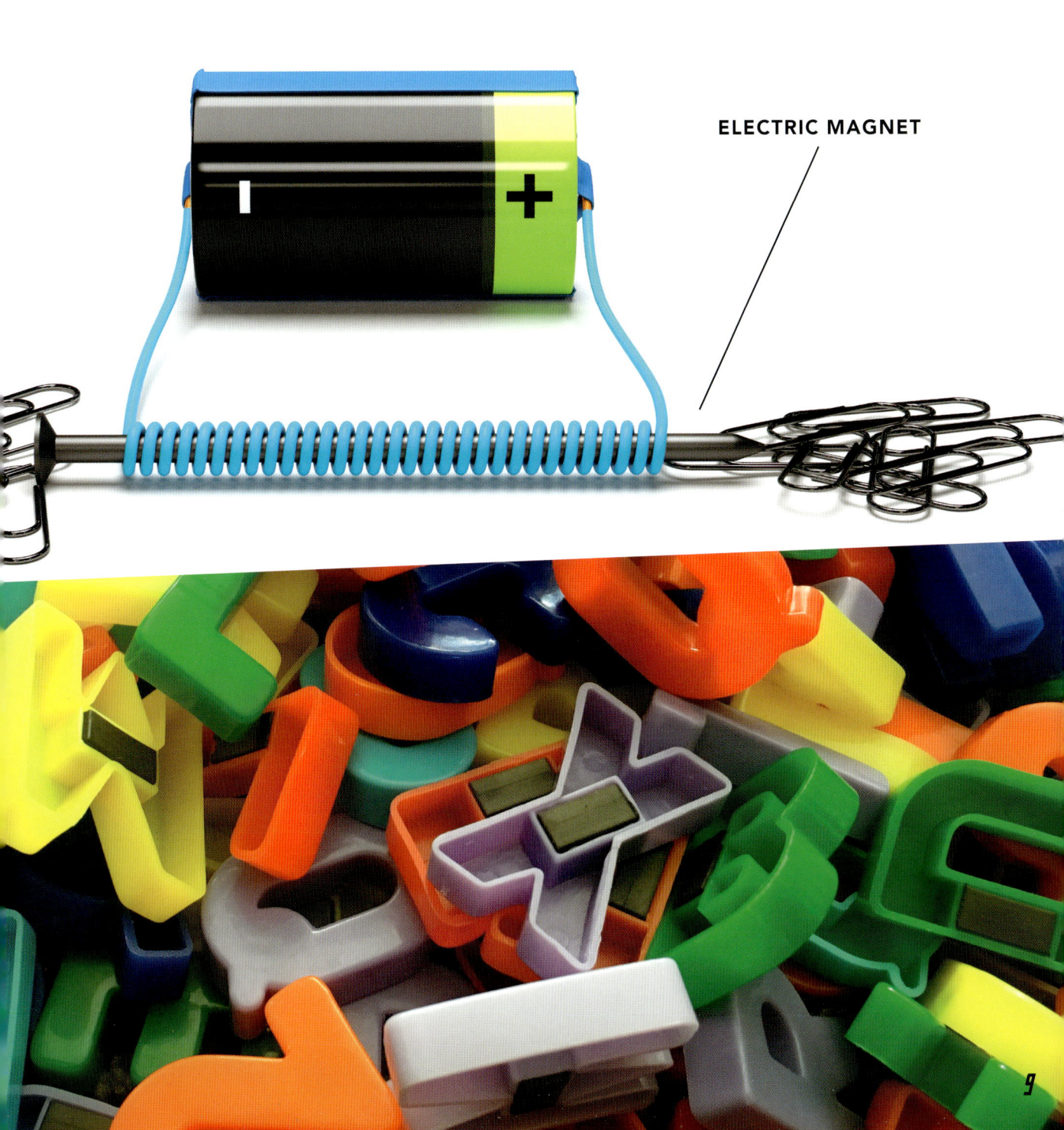
ELECTRIC MAGNET

MAGNETIC POLES

A magnet has two ends called **poles**. These areas have the strongest magnetic field. There is a north pole and a south pole. Opposite poles pull together. Matching poles push away from each other. For example, a north and south pole will pull together. But two south poles will always push apart.

pole one of the two ends of a magnet

NORTH AND SOUTH

More than 1,000 years ago, the first **compass** was made in China. It was a needle that acted as a magnet floating in a bowl of water. The needle always lined up in the north-south direction.

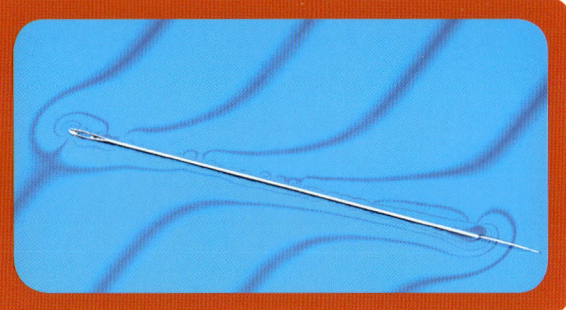

opposite poles pull together

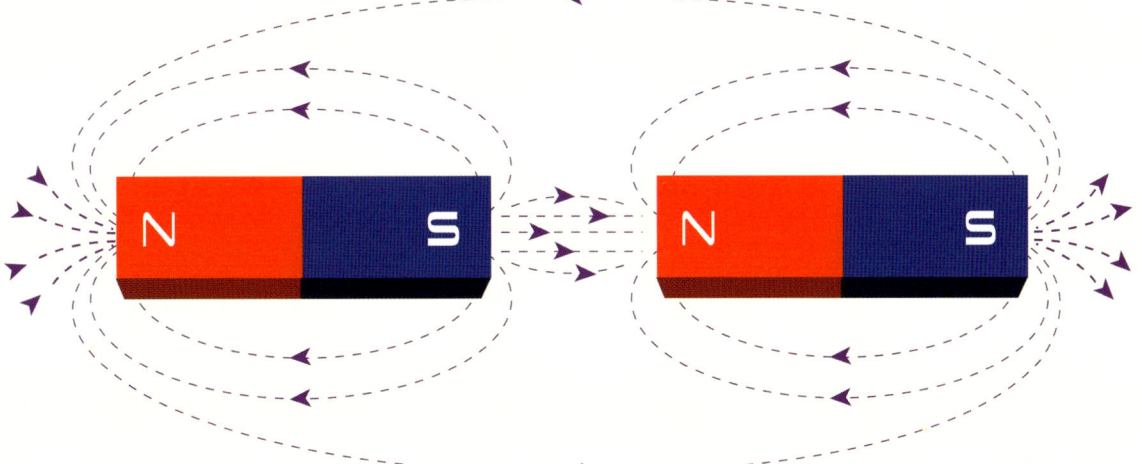

matching poles push apart

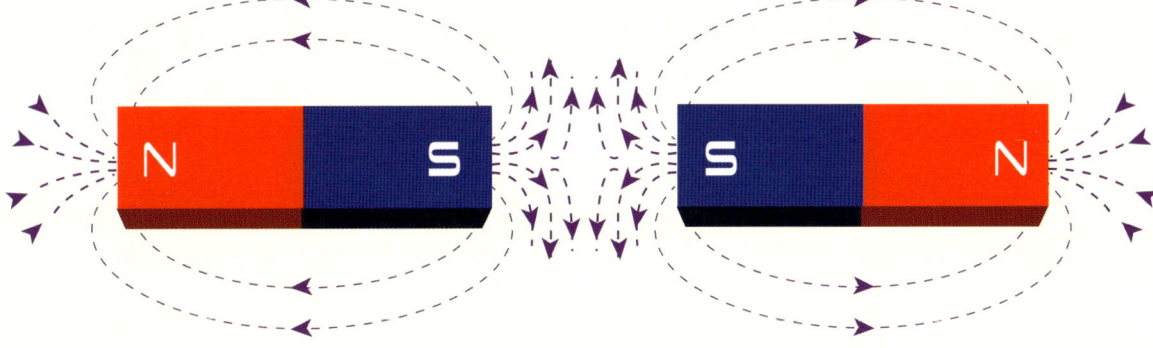

compass instrument used for finding directions

MAGNETIC MATERIALS

Some materials are attracted to magnets. Iron, nickel, cobalt and most types of steel are common magnetic materials. This is why magnets stick to steel fridge doors. But they do not stick to wood or plastic doors.

FACT

One of the world's strongest magnets is in Florida, USA. It is stronger than 4,000 ordinary magnets. Powerful magnets such as this are used to study medicine and computers.

TRAVEL ON A
MAGLEV TRAIN

Maglev trains move very fast. They do this by using magnets. Two sets of magnets move the train. One set of magnets pushes the train up. When the train is "floating", another set of magnets moves the train forward.

FACT

A maglev train in Japan is the fastest in the world. The train whizzes by at 602 kilometres (374 miles) per hour.

ELECTRIC CARS

The electric motor in an electric car uses magnetism. The motor has a set of magnets. The magnets push and pull on a loop connected to a shaft. The shaft turns the wheels of the car. This **cycle** repeats again and again, making the car move forward.

cycle set of events that happen over and over again

FACT
Electric cars are becoming more popular. There are now more than 1 million electric cars in Europe.

MAKING NOISE

Speakers use magnets to make sounds. Each speaker has two magnets. The first one uses electricity. The second one does not. The first magnet gets stronger when a lot of electricity flows through it. These magnets work together to make a cone in the speaker move back and forth. The movement creates sound waves that we can hear.

CAN YOU HEAR ME?

Speakers can be found in many places and in many things. Sound systems have big speakers. Mobile phones have tiny ones. Stadiums and cinemas have speakers. Where else can speakers be found?

MAGNETISM EXPERIMENT

WHAT DOES A MAGNET ATTRACT?

MATERIALS:

- bowl of small objects such as safety pins, marbles, erasers, paper clips, sweets and keys
- string
- large magnet

WHAT TO DO:

1. Make a list of the objects in the bowl.

2. Make a prediction about what will happen when you lower the magnet into the bowl. What objects will cling to the magnet? What objects will not? Write, draw or say your prediction.

3. Tie a string around the magnet. Then lower the magnet into the bowl and move it around. Observe what happens. What objects cling to the magnet?

4. Check your prediction. How does what you observed compare to your prediction?

GLOSSARY

compass instrument for finding directions

current movement of electrical charges in a certain direction

cycle set of events that happen over and over again

electron one of the tiny particles that make up an atom

magnetism natural force of a magnet that pulls it to iron or steel

magnetic field area around a magnet or electrical current that can produce a force on other objects

pole one of the two ends of a magnet

FIND OUT MORE

BOOKS

All About Physics (Big Questions), Richard Hammond (DK Children, 2015)

Experiments with Magnets (Read and Experiment), Isabel Thomas (Raintree, 2016)

Magnetism (Essential Physical Science), Louise and Richard Spilsbury (Raintree, 2014)

WEBSITES

www.bbc.com/bitesize/articles/zpvcrdm
Learn more about magnets.

www.dkfindout.com/uk/science/magnets
Find out more about magnets.

COMPREHENSION QUESTIONS

1. How do people know that an invisible magnetic field surrounds a magnet? Use words and phrases from this book to support your answer.

2. This book discusses many uses for magnets. How would you use magnets?

3. What machine could you make from two bar magnets? What type of work would your machine do? Make sure you explain how the magnets make your machine work.

INDEX

compasses 11
currents 6

electricity 8, 18
electric motors 16, 17
electrons 6

force 4, 6

maglev trains 14
magnetic fields 6, 7, 10
magnetic materials 12
movement 4, 6, 10, 11, 14, 16, 18

permanent magnets 8
poles 10

sounds 18

temporary magnets 8